Alice in Wonderland

a play

Based on the books by Lewis Carroll

Adapted by Holly Beardsley

Alice in Wonderland ©Holly Beardsley 2017

Those interested in performance rights should apply at HollyBeardsley.com

For further information contact
Holly@HollyBeardsley.com

As Always,
for Janet & John

Table of Contents

Cast of Characters

Alice

Ada

White Rabbit

Dinah

Cheshire Cat

Cheshire Cat 2

Cheshire Cat 3

Cheshire Cat 4

Cheshire Cat 5

Cheshire Cat 6

Cheshire Cat 7

Cheshire Cat 8

Cheshire Cat 9

Mouse

Tweedle Dum

Tweedle Dee

Mad Hatter

Frog Footman

Dodo

Canary

Songbird

Eaglet

Magpie

Parrot

Owl

White Queen

White Knight

Queen of Spades

Queen of Diamonds

Queen of Clubs

Cuckoo Bird

Caterpillar

March Hare

Dormouse

Rose

Lily

Chrysanthemum

Daffodil

Poppy

Violet

Amaryllis

Jasmine

Petal

Marigold

Iris

Daisy

Baby's Breath

Carnation

Fern

Red Queen

Red Rook 1

Red Rook 2

Red Pawns

Red Bishops

Red Knights

Kangaroo Barrister

Chef

Cards

Two of Spades

Three of Spades*

Four of Spades*

Five of Spades*

Six of Spades

Seven of Spades *

Eight of Spades

Nine of Spades

Ten of Spades

Jack of Spades

King of Spades

Two of Diamonds*

Three of Diamonds*

Four of Diamonds*

Five of Diamonds

Six of Diamonds *

Seven of Diamonds

Eight of Diamonds*

Nine of Diamonds*

Ten of Diamonds*

Jack of Diamonds*

King of Diamonds

Two of Clubs
Three of Clubs*

Four of Clubs*

Five of Clubs

Six of Clubs

Seven of Clubs*

Eight of Clubs*

Nine of Clubs

Ten of Clubs*

Jack of Clubs

King of Clubs

Speaking Card

Prelude: Wonderland Ballet Laughs

We open to find ALL the Wonderland characters in a large ballet formation. They are grouped by parts such as: FLOWERS, CARDS, ROYAL CARDS, CHESS PIECES, BIRDS, MAD HATTER's party, as well as individual parts like KANGAROO, FROG FOOTMAN, and the CHEF. MUSIC, The Pizzicati by Leo Delibes plays. At each pause in the music, a character tells a joke. ALL laugh. After the laughter, the music starts again and they dance.

This dance is an introduction to Wonderland, and many of the characters that we will not see again until Act 2.

Dance
Pause 0:06
SEVEN of SPADES: Why did the man refuse to play cards on safari?
THREE of CLUBS : Because there were too many cheetahs.
Laugh, then dance.

Pause 0:11
FOUR of DIAMONDS & FOUR of CLUBS:Why didn't the two 4's feel like dinner?
EIGHT of SPADES: Because they already 8.
Laugh, then dance.

Pause 0:14

MAD HATTER: What did one hat say to the other?

MARCH HARE: You stay here, I'll go on a head.

Laugh, then dance.

Pause 0:18

NINE of DIAMONDS: How can you get four suits for a dollar?

SEVEN of CLUBS : Buy a deck of cards.

Laugh, then dance.

Pause 0:24

OWL: Why does Humpty Dumpty love autumn?

EAGLET: Because Humpty Dumpty had a great fall.

Laugh, then dance.

Pause 0:28

RED ROOK 1: How did the playing card beat the chess piece?

TEN of DIAMONDS: Because paper beats rook.

Laugh, then dance.

Pause 0:31

 FROG FOOTMAN: What starts with E, ends with E, and has only 1 letter in it? *(Pause)* An Envelope.

Laugh, then dance.

Pause 0:37

SEVEN of SPADES : Why is the number six so scared?

SIX of DIAMONDS: Because seven eight nine!

Laugh, then dance.

Pause 0:52

POPPY: What kind of flowers are on your face?

DAISY: Tulips!

Laugh, then dance.

Pause 0:57

SIX of DIAMONDS: What is the playing cards favorite dance move?

SPADES 3, 4, & 5: The shuffle.

Laugh, then dance.

Pause 0:59

SIX of CLUBS : What did the poker player say to his hand?

FIVE of CLUBS: I can't deal with you anymore.

Laugh, then dance.

Pause 1:10

CHESHIRE CAT 2: What do you get if you cross a cat with a lemon?

CHESHIRE CAT 3: A sour-puss.

Laugh, then dance.

Pause 1:13

CHESHIRE CAT 4: What is smarter than a talking cat?

CHESHIRE CAT 5: A spelling bee.

Laugh, then dance.

Pause 1:16

KANGAROO BARRISTER: Can a Kangaroo jump as high as the Empire State building? *(Pause)* Of course! Buildings can't jump!
Laugh, then dance.

Pause 1:24
MOUSE: What stays in one corner but travels around the world?
MAD HATTER: No idea.
MARCH HARE: Not a clue.
FROG FOOTMAN: A stamp.
Laugh, then dance.

Pause 1:28
CHEF: A man told me an onion is the only food that makes you cry, so I threw a coconut at his face. *(Pause)* He was wrong.
Laugh, then dance.

Pause 1:40
CHESHIRE CAT 6: A cat swallows a ball of yarn…
CHESHIRE CAT 7: Then what happens?
CHESHIRE CAT 8: She has a litter of mittens.

Pause 1:45
CHEF: Knock, knock
THREE of DIAMONDS: Who's there?
CHEF: Etch.
THREE of DIAMONDS: Etch who?

CHEF: Guzzenheight.

Dance.

Pause 1:50.

WHITE RABBIT: *(Entering SL)* Knock. Knock.

ALL: Who's there?

WHITE RABBIT: The White Rabbit.

ALL: The White Rabbit who?

WHITE RABBIT: You know who I am— Get backstage! The show's about to start!

Dance.

Freeze in pose.

Then exit.

ACT ONE

Scene 1

A DAISY FIELD, performed in front of curtain. ADA and ALICE sit in a clump of white and yellow daisies DSL. ADA, the older and more mature teacher, sits on a small stool or stump and reads to her sister from a book. While ALICE, in her boredom, sits with her legs crossed, and makes a daisy chain around her tiny cat, Dinah. Dinah is represented by a stuffed animal cat with a large pink bow around her neck. Curtain is slightly open at center, leaving a sliver of darkness.

ADA: Now, Alice, pay attention to your lesson. *(Reading aloud)* Lady's etiquette for dinner, rule #14, Stuff not your mouth so much as to fill your cheeks, but be content with small mouthfuls. And chew like you have a secret.

ALICE: What kind of secret?

ADA: Rule # 15. Smell not your food, nor flip it upside down upon your plate to inspect the other side.

ALICE: *(Sighing)* Is it tea time yet, Ada?

ADA: *(Ignoring, she reads on)* Rule # 16. Blow not your food when too hot, but wait, *(pause)* with patience, till it becomes cool.

ALICE: *(Big sigh, then up on her knees, in perfect imitation of ADA)* Rule # 17. Blow not the wind from your seat, but wait, *(pause)* till the end of the meal. When it's polite.

ADA: *(Aghast)* Alice! *(Laughing)* Young ladies should not say such things! Imagine what your husband will think!

ALICE: *(It is her turn to be aghast)* My husband?! I don't have a husband. I'm just a girl!

ADA: Maybe not now, my dear. But you will. You will have a husband, and children and—

ALICE: When?

ADA: When you grow up.

ALICE: I will not. I will not grow up.

ADA: *(Laughing again)* But you must! It is the way of the world.

ALICE: *(Standing defiantly)* Not in my world. In my world, there are no husbands, or wives but Kings and Queens—

ADA: There is only one Queen at a time. You know that from your history lesson—

ALICE: And no lessons, just games! Never-ending games of cards, and chess, and croquet—

ADA: Games *must* end sometime—

ALICE: *(Ignoring)* And in my world, it's tea time, ALL the time!

ADA: What nonsense, Alice!

ALICE: *(With delight)* Yes! Utter nonsense! *(Picking up Dinah, and beginning to dance with her)* And all the animals, the trees, and the flowers, will walk, and talk, and dance— especially dance! And wear gloves, of course. That's only good manners, Dinah.

DINAH: *(from offstage)* Meow.

ALICE: Not "Meow," Dinah. You say, "Yes, Miss Alice."

DINAH: *(Offstage)* Meow.

ADA: Well, it's a man's world, I'm afraid. And in a man's world — *(She picks up another book)* we learn about geography. *(She pats the ground next to her)* Come sit by me, and we'll talk about far off places, like New Zealand.

ALICE: Oh, but Geography is so *very dry.* It's practically dusty.

ADA: *(Opening her book)* Then perhaps we will learn about the Nile.

ALICE sits down next to ADA with another bored sigh. Then from offstage we hear the WHITE RABBIT acting as a narrator.

WHITE RABBIT: *(Offstage)* Alice was beginning to grow very tired sitting next to her sister on the bank, with nothing to do but her lessons. Once or twice she peeped into the book her sister was reading—

ADA: *(Reading aloud)* Owing to the precise longitude and latitude of cartographers, the exact position of the Nile is—

ALICE sighs loudly falling over from boredom. As WHITE RABBIT continues, she rolls onto her stomach crossing her legs behind her, and begins to daydream, rolling a daisy between her fingers.

WHITE RABBIT: *(Still offstage)* But the book had no pictures and no conversations in it—
ALICE: *(Aside to audience)* What is the point of a book with no pictures and conversations in it?

WHITE RABBIT: *(Still offstage)* So she began wondering, as well as she could wonder, for the hot day was making her feel very sleepy... She was wondering whether the pleasure of making another daisy chain was worth getting up to pick more daisies... when she spotted a white rabbit in a waistcoat, racing by with his pocket watch out.

ALICE gasps at the sight of the WHITE RABBIT, as he enters DSL. She and ADA freeze, ALICE looking at the WHITE RABBIT and ADA still reading her book.

WHITE RABBIT: *(To audience)* Who am I? Why, I am the White Rabbit, of course. And this, *(he poses to show off his vest)* is my waistcoat— and this is my watch. *(He pulls a pocket watch from his vest and is suddenly startled by the time.)* Oh my! Oh dear! I'm late! *(To audience again)* We're late, *very* late. There's a lot of story to get to, two volumes full, impossible, lovely nonsense, cards, chess, croquet, and tea time, of course. So— *(Pause, then with a knowing smile)* Follow me… down the rabbit hole…

WHITE RABBIT darts into the center of the Curtain.

ALICE: *(Picking up the stuffed animal)* Come, Dinah! Let's chase him! Mr. Rabbit! Oh, Mr. Rabbit!

ALICE follows the RABBIT into the curtains as fantastical music rises and lights dim through scene change.

Scene 2

The curtain opens partially as if revealing a cross section of the deep, dark rabbit hole. WHITE RABBIT appears in front of the red curtain DSR this time. While WHITE RABBIT speaks ALICE crawls up and stands on a two to three foot tall black platform as if she is floating in space. A fan and lights beneath her, give her the appearance of falling down the "rabbit hole."

WHITE RABBIT: The rabbit hole went straight on like a tunnel for some way, and then dipped suddenly down, so suddenly that Alice had not a moment to think before she found herself falling down a deep well.

Props on long sticks move from the ground, past ALICE, giving the impression that she is falling next to the strange items WHITE RABBIT describes. The sticks are being manipulated by Wonderland Shadows. They continue to "fall past her" until the lights black out.

WHITE RABBIT: Either the well was very deep, or she fell very slowly, for she had plenty of time as she went down to look about her and wonder what was to happen next. She floated by all manner of things, books on shelves, maps on pegs, and even, a glass jar of Orange Marmalade.

ALICE: *(Taking the jar "out of the air")* Oh! Orange Marmalade!

WHITE RABBIT: It was empty.

ALICE: Empty. *(She sighs and "puts it back" by releasing it in the air. Wonderland Shadow pulls it offstage.)* Well, after a fall such as this, I shall think of nothing of falling down stairs. *(After a moment)* I wonder how many miles I have fallen by this time? Perhaps, I will fall right through the center of the earth! Wherever will I come out? Hmm, that surely depends on the latitude, or is it the longitude?

WHITE RABBIT: Alice had no idea what latitude was, or longitude either, but thought they were nice big words to say in case someone was listening.

ALICE: How funny it will be to come out where people walk where their heads ought to be— New Zealand, perhaps? Or is it the Falkland Islands?

WHITE RABBIT: Alice was rather glad no one was listening this time, as that didn't sound right at all.

ALICE: New Guinea?

DINAH: *(Still represented by a stuffed animal, falls from above while she yowls from offstage.)* Meeeoooooaaaahhhhhhhhhhhh!!!! *(Caught by a Wonderland Shadow)*

ALICE: Dinah! Dinah, was that you?!

WHITE RABBIT: Dinah, was the cat, if you recall.

ALICE: Are you falling too? I'm afraid there's no milk in this rabbit hole, nor saucers neither... Or any mice for you to chase... Forget about orange marmalade, Dinah, that jar's empty. I know you're just a kitten but maybe you could catch a bat... Do cats eat bats?

WHITE RABBIT: And here Alice began to be very sleepy, imagining herself walking hand in hand with Dear Dinah and asking her—

ALICE: *(Sleepy)* Tell me truthfully, now. Have you ever ate a bat?

WHITE RABBIT: When suddenly—

Lights blackout. We hear a thud, bicycle horn, cat screech, cymbal crash, and then ALICE gives a very loud "Ooumph!" Lights come back on and the platform is gone. ALICE lays flat on her back with her feet in the air; a very comical sight with the large amount of crinoline and victorian bloomers she wears. There is also a new narrator. The first CHESHIRE CAT appears opposite of the WHITE RABBIT, DSL. He should be lounging on something, very catlike.

WHITE RABBIT opens his mouth to speak but the CHESHIRE CAT speaks first.

CHESHIRE CAT 1: *(Cooly)* Down she came, like a down feather pillow, like a sheep on its back, like— *(looking at ALICE, then the WHITE RABBIT, then the audience, he smiles)* — well, not like a cat, that's for sure.

WHITE RABBIT: *(Annoyed)* That was my line, Cheshire Cat.

CHESHIRE CAT 1: Aren't you late for something?

WHITE RABBIT: *(Looking at his watch, he gives a startled yelp)* Oh, my ears and whiskers! It's getting so late!

CHESHIRE CAT 1: Go ahead, we've got it from here.

WHITE RABBIT: *(Bouncing to go)* Well, just make sure you stay on book! None of that anachronistic new stuff! No breaking the fourth wall! And absolutely, under no circumstance, will there be any more audience participation!

CHESHIRE CAT 1: We wouldn't dream of it. *(He chuckles softly, licking his paw.)*
WHITE RABBIT: Oh! I must go, I'm late, I'm late, I'm late! *(He darts through the curtain and exits.)*

CHESHIRE CAT 1: *(After a moment, he looks directly at an audience member, cooly)* Wound a little tight, don't you think?

ALICE: *(Sitting up)* Where am I?

CHESHIRE CAT 1: From another perspective, mine, the question might be, "Who are you?"

ALICE: *(Repeating the question)* "Who are you?" ?

CHESHIRE CAT 1: I am the Cheshire Cat. And you? *(After a beat)* Perhaps you should ask yourself, "Who am I?"

ALICE: "Who am I?" ?

CHESHIRE CAT 1: I can't answer all the questions, dear. You must know who *you* are.

ALICE: I'm afraid, I'm not sure. I knew who I was this morning but so much has happened since then. *(Touching her head)* I know I am not Ada for her hair has much longer ringlets than mine. Oh, I hope I'm not Mabel, she is frightfully stupid. I can't be Mabel because I know all sorts of things... Perhaps I should test myself— Times table? Geography? London is the capital of Paris, and Paris is the capital of Rome, and Rome is the capital— Oh no! That's not right at all!

CHESHIRE CAT 1. *(Pointing DSR)* Maybe you should ask her...

ALICE: Ask who? Mabel?

Curtains open to reveal eight doors of different sizes, shapes, and colors, all standing in a row just downstage of a second curtain. The doors are cartoonish in design, with extra large keyholes and knobs. The door closest to CSL is a dutch style door that opens into two halves.

In front of the doors, DSR, stands a cat, a kitten, really, for she is very small. Different than the Cheshire Cat, she is dressed all in black, with white gloves, and a white bib apron, tied just above her black tail, like the markings on a black and white cat. She wears "cat eye" glasses and a pink bow around her neck or in her hair. ALICE recognizes the pink bow and gasps, for this cat, is her cat, Dinah. DINAH stands looking bewildered with her hands out to steady herself.

ALICE: Dinah! Dinah is that you?!

DINAH: Miss Alice? *(Looking up the rabbit hole)* What was that?

ALICE: You can talk!

DINAH: Of course, I can talk. *(Confused)* Maybe it's you who's learned to meow?

ALICE: That's nonsense Dinah, I should know if I was meowing.

CHESHIRE CAT 2: *(Stepping out from behind a door, she says 'meow' like 'now.')* Would you, meow?

ALICE: Oh, look, another cat! Who does she belong to?

DINAH: *(Still a little ruffled from the fall, she licks her paw)* Why must she belong to anyone?

CHESHIRE CAT 1: She is the Cheshire Cat.

ALICE: I thought you were the Cheshire Cat?

The CHESHIRE CATS slink out from behind the doors in feline fashion, one right after the other.

CHESHIRE CAT 3: He is.
CHESHIRE CAT 4: They both are
CHESHIRE CAT 5: I am too.
CHESHIRE CAT 6: So am I.
CHESHIRE CAT 7: I am also the Cheshire Cat.
CHESHIRE CAT 8 & 9: We all are.

ALICE: How can you *all* be the Cheshire Cat?

CHESHIRE CAT 1: You've heard of a Cat with nine lives, yes?

ALICE: Yes, but you rarely see nine cats living just one life between them.

CHESHIRE CAT 3: We're saving Time.
CHESHIRE CAT 4: He greatly appreciates it, you know.
CHESHIRE CAT 5: So many people are often cursing Time.
CHESHIRE CAT 6: Calling him a thief.
CHESHIRE CAT 7: Just murdering him!
CHESHIRE CAT 8 & 9: We prefer to save Time.

CHESHIRE CAT 1: *(After a moment)* He's a great guy, Time. Loves to laugh.

ALICE: *(Surrounded by the CATS)* Uh... I suppose that's kind of you. Would you do me the kindness of telling me which way I am to go from here?

CHESHIRE CAT 2: That depends a great deal—
CHESHIRE CAT 3: On where you want to go?

ALICE: I don't much care where—

CHESHIRE CAT 8: Then it doesn't matter—
CHESHIRE CAT 9: which way you go—

ALICE: *(As an explanation)* So long as I end up somewhere.

CHESHIRE CAT 1: Oh, you're sure to do that... If only you walk long enough.

ALICE: How do *you* know?

CHESHIRE CAT 1: I'm a cat. I can see the future. All cats do. That is why we nap so much. When you already know what's going to happen... *(Yawning)* there is no need to kick up such a fuss.

CHESHIRE CAT 2: Yes, yes.
CHESHIRE CAT 3: WE—
CHESHIRE CAT 4: SEE—
CHESHIRE CAT 5: ALL.

CHESHIRE CAT 6: Know all!

CHESHIRE CAT 7: Horrible Mess!

CHESHIRE CAT 8: Just ask Grumpy Cat.

CHESHIRE CAT 9: *(After a beat)* He knew too much.

They all nod in agreement.

DINAH: They're right. Although to be fair... *(She gestures at the whole of the stage)* I did not see this coming... I am just a kitten though.

CHESHIRE CAT 1: That's our cue.

He gets up to go. CHESHIRE CATS speak as they turn to exit.

CHESHIRE CAT 2: Yes, yes.

CHESHIRE CAT 3: We—

CHESHIRE CAT 4: are—

CHESHIRE CAT 5: late—

CHESHIRE CAT 6: for a game of croquet!

CHESHIRE CAT 7: With the cards—

CHESHIRE CAT 8: And the Red Queen!

CHESHIRE CAT 9: *(After a beat)* Watch your head!

ALICE: Wait, wait! I have questions! Where are we? Where did the White Rabbit go? What's going to happen next?

CHESHIRE CAT 1: The White Rabbit went through the door, of course.

ALICE: Which door?

CHESHIRE CAT 1: Oh! And— *(Turning back just before exit)* Drink me. Eat me. And don't forget the key! *(He exits.)*

ALICE: But where am I?

CHESHIRE CAT 1: *(Offstage, whispers slowly, cooly)* You're..in..Wonderland…

DINAH: Woah...that was creepy.

Scene 3

(Continuing Scene 2 with no blackout in between scenes.)

ALICE: Drink me? Eat me? What does that mean?

During the following, a MOUSE in a smart little vest and enormous glasses enters DSR. Despite his smart little vest and enormous glasses, he still acts like a normal mouse. Looking for cheese, etc.

DINAH: And don't forget the key... *(She suddenly notices MOUSE. She quietly gasps. Then starts the long process of pouncing, comically wiggling with anticipation—)*

ALICE: *(Looking about, not noticing DINAH or MOUSE.)* Alright, well we just have to stay calm, and think this out. This is a strange place, Dinah. So we must take care not to be distracted. I know that you are just a kitten but—

MOUSE suddenly sees DINAH and gasps— MOUSE freezes, DINAH freezes. ALICE turns and sees them both.

ALICE: Is that a—

DINAH: MOUSE!

MOUSE screams as he runs and DINAH chases him, they both dart off DSL.

ALICE: Well then, Alice. You're all by yourself now... *(She starts to sniffle.)* Oh no! You cannot cry! Get yourself together, Alice! You can't go falling apart here. Who knows where you'll end up? *(Collecting herself, she restates her situation.)* The White Rabbit went through one of these doors, but which?

Suddenly the FROG FOOTMAN comes through a door SR. He wears a regal livery, powdered wig, and holds an enormous envelope.

ALICE: *(Pointing at the door he just entered)* Pardon me — uh, sir. Did you happen to see a White Rabbit go through that door?
FROG FOOTMAN: That door's locked. And there's no use knocking, I'm on the same side as you are.
ALICE: But did you see a White Rabbit? With a waistcoat? And a pocket watch?
FROG FOOTMAN: There might be some sense in you knocking if the door were between us. For instance if you were inside, you could knock, and I could let you out. But as we are both on this side of the door. I cannot help you. *(After a beat)* I have an invitation I must deliver. It is from the Queen. To play croquet.
ALICE: Then that's a no. About the White Rabbit?
FROG FOOTMAN looks at her, says nothing, then exits SR.

ALICE: How strange...

She turns back, passing by the doors, she comes upon a small table. On the table are three items— a bottle, a piece of a cake, and a key.

What's this? *(She picks up the key.)* It's a key! It must open one of these doors. Maybe it's the door the rabbit went through. *(Looking at the doors)* But these keyholes are all too big.

ALICE looks through the keyhole on the door closest CSL. There is a feminine scream and the MAD HATTER throws open the top half of the dutch door. Just inside the door is a comical shower curtain, the MAD HATTER leans outside the door clutching the shower curtain around himself as if he is naked. And in true MAD HATTER fashion, he wears a marvelous shower themed top hat.

MAD HATTER: Do you mind?!

ALICE: Oh, I am very sorry!

MAD HATTER: Very Sorry, what an odd name!

ALICE: *(Stammering)* I'm sorry— wait, what—?

MAD HATTER: I know *you're* Sorry, you already said that. What I don't know is why you were peeping in my keyhole? *(He brings a cup of tea out of the shower, sips it and brings it back behind the curtain.)*

ALICE: I wasn't peeping! I was just looking for the white rabbit.

MAD HATTER: Is that what they call it these days?... Well.. what did you say your name was again? Oh yes, Very Sorry. *(To Audience)* What a strange name... must be French... Well, Very Sorry, you won't find him in here!

ALICE: No, no, of course not— But I'm not "Very Sorry."

MAD HATTER: You're not sorry? That's a bit rude, don't you think?! You burst in on me in the shower without a hint of remorse!

ALICE: No, no, no— *My name* is Alice, you see? Please, there is no need to be so mad.

MAD HATTER: But I am mad, You-See. I am the MAD HATTER. *(He removes his hat, tilting it toward her. He puts it back.)* We're all mad here.

ALICE: *(Aside to audience)* I've noticed. *(Back to MH)* I was just trying to follow the White Rabbit. He went through one of these doors. I have a key, but it's too small for any of these keyholes...

MAD HATTER: Try behind the curtain.

ALICE pauses for a second, looks at the audience, back to MH, then points at the shower curtain, as if to say, "May I?"

MAD HATTER: Not my curtain! Nosey. The other curtain! Center Stage!

MAD HATTER shuts the top half of the door in her face. ALICE moves to center stage, pulling back the curtain. Behind it is a large scenery flat with a tiny door ten inches tall built three quarters to the top of the flat. There is also a tiny stairway leading up to the door.

ALICE: Aha! A door! Let's give the key a try. *(She puts the key into the door)* It fits!

There is ratcheting sound as she turns the key and the door unlocks. The door opens and a bright light shines out from behind it, like it's a beautiful sunny day just behind it.

During the following, MOUSE comes back, panting and out of breath. He looks over his shoulder for DINAH. Seeing, that he's lost her, he breathes a sigh of relief.

ALICE: It works! It works! Oh, and there's a beautiful garden on the other side...and there's the rabbit! Hello, Mr. Rabbit! Hello!... Oh, but the door! Oh no, the door is much too small. I could get my head in perhaps, but it would be of no use to me without my shoulders. How will I ever get through?!

MOUSE, still panting, notices the table with the bottle and the cake. He picks up the bottle.

MOUSE: *(Reading the tag on the bottle)* Drink me. Well, I am very thirsty.

MOUSE starts to tilt the bottle back to drink it. ALICE whips around, remembering the Cheshire Cat's first instruction, "Drink me."

ALICE: Wait! That's mine!

MOUSE: *(Reading the tag again)* Drink me? Is that your name?... *(To Audience)* What an odd name.... Must be French.

ALICE: *(Frustrated)* No. That is *not* my name. It was an instruction given to me by the Cheshire Cat—

MOUSE: *(Gasping)* Did you say— *(Pointing offstage at an incoming DINAH, he yells in fear)* CAAAAAaaaaaTTTTT!!!!

MOUSE throws the bottle in the air in fear, whipping around to run, as DINAH comes streaming onto the stage. She yells a kitten yowl of glee, as she runs MOUSE off the stage. And ALICE catches the bottle.

ALICE: Really, Dinah! ... Oh, I shall never get through the door at this rate. *(Reading)* Drink me...

TWEEDLE DEE steps out opposite of ALICE, downstage in a separate pool of light. He speaks like he is in a catchy 1950's commercial.

TWEEDLE DEE: *(To audience)* Are you tired of not fitting in? Tired of being too big in your own body? Would you like to be lighter? Smaller? ... Are you just too big to fit through the door?

TWEEDLE DEE still looks at audience, frozen, waiting for a response. ALICE steps forward in line with TWEEDLE DEE.

ALICE: Uh... yes?

TWEEDLE DEE: Then try— "DRINK ME!" Guaranteed to make you smaller, lighter— just one sip, and you will literally shrink.

ALICE: Oh! Well, that seems to be exactly what I am looking for....

After a moment, the light fades around TWEEDLE DEE and he exits.

During the following, ALICE thoughtfully walks behind the table. Behind the table, there is a small alcove partition, hidden with the same fabric as the table cloth. She steps into the alcove preparing to shrink by "give it a taste."

ALICE: *(Looking at the bottle)* Ada would say that I should check the bottle for the words "poison" or "beware!" Certainly, if you drink a bottle marked poison, it's bound to disagree with you sooner or later. *(Checking it over)* … Well, perhaps I ought to give it a taste.

On each description she abruptly shrinks an inch, squatting down into the alcove. Finally she drops behind the table after "Hot buttered toast." A slide whistle noise goes down, representing the rest of her shrinking to nothing more than a little fairy light.

ALICE: Yumm! It tastes like cherry tart… *(Dropping, then another sip)* … Lemon custard…*(Dropping, then another sip)*... Roast Beef and *(Dropping, then another sip)* Hot buttered toast. Woooahhh! *(She hides behind the table. Slide whistle.)*

During the following, a small fairy spotlight representing shrunken ALICE comes out from behind the table and begins to ascend the steps up to the small door.

ALICE: Oh my! I must be the size of a little fairy. *(The LIGHT does a happy little dance)* How delightful! Well, there is no time to waste. I shall go up the stairs and through the door to find the White Rabbit.

Light begins to delicately dance up the staircase leading to the small door. Just then DINAH enters SR out of breath, she's lost the mouse again. Suddenly she sees the light, quietly gasps, and begins the comical process of pouncing once more, wiggling with anticipation. Finally, with a yowl, she pounces on the light! During the following, DINAH and "Alice" do an elaborate dance with DINAH chasing and pouncing after

*the light. She ends with "Alice" hiding under the table for
protection.*

ALICE: Dinah! Dinah, no! You naughty kitty! No, it's Alice! It's
Miss Alice!

*TWEEDLE DUM steps out opposite of ALICE and DINAH,
downstage in a separate pool of light. He too speaks like he is
in a catchy 1950's commercial.*

TWEEDLE DUM: *(To audience)* Problems too big for you? In
over your head? Do you need a leg up? A hand? A foot?
Several feet— are you, perhaps, hiding under a table?

*TWEEDLE DUM still looks at audience, frozen, waiting for a
response. ALICE shouts from under the table.*

ALICE: Yes! Help me!

TWEEDLE DUM: Then try— "EAT ME!" Just one bite and you
will be longer, taller... no longer under the table!

ALICE: But the cake is *on* the table! How am I going to get it
from here?

*DINAH, her attention drawn to the cake on the table, cocks
her head to the side, then swiftly knocks the cake plate off the
table, sending it skittering offstage.*

ALICE: *(After a beat)* You really are such a cat, aren't you Dinah? … *(DINAH shrugs)*... Oh, I better run for it… Here I go!

LIGHT comes on just outside the table and speeds off after the cake plate. DINAH attempts to pounce and misses.

DINAH: Oh! Missed it!

ALICE: *(From offstage)* Here it is… just one bite?

TWEEDLE DUM: *(Still looking at the audience)* Just one bite!

ALICE: *(From offstage, muffles eating sounds)* Oh my! It's chocolate, my favorite! Oh my, it's delicious!

TWEEDLE DUM: *(Looking uneasy)* Just ONE bite! Only one!

ALICE: Oh my! Oh no! What's happening to me?! I'm growing too much!

TWEEDLE DUM and DINAH back Upstage LEFT, looking up as a slide whistle noise goes up. Suddenly an enormous black MaryJane slipper shoe and stocking, Alice's "foot", comes out SR.

TWEEDLE DUM: *(Losing the 1950's commercial tone with a bit of panic)* I told you just one bite!

DINAH: *(Finally noticing, it's ALICE)* Miss Alice! You're big again! Oh my, you're very big!

TWEEDLE DEE: *(Entering in behind TWEEDLE DUM, looking up)* Look what you did, Dummy! Didn't you tell her just one bite?! She's only supposed to eat one bite!

TWEEDLE DUM: I did, I told her!

ALICE: Oh no! Now I'll never fit through the door! *(She sniffs, starting to cry.)* I can't go home like this either. I'm three times the size of Ada. I can't be her LITTLE sister like this! Oh no! *(Crying)* Oh no! Oh no! Oh no!

DINAH: Now don't go crying Miss Alice! You're so big your tears are likely to drown us all!

ALICE: *(Starting to sob)* I can't help it! Everything's so topsy turvy here! *(Crying)* I can't get a hold of myself one bit! *(Crying)* Waaahhh!!!

CHESHIRE CATS 2- 5 run from SR to SL holding blue yards of fabric, CHESHIRE CATS 6-9 step out SR holding the other end of the fabrics. The CATS begin to move the blue fabric up and down like it is an ocean. CATS mock ALICE as she cries, making big "Boo hoo" faces at the audience. They slowly move the fabric up simulating gathering water. TWEEDLE DEE, TWEEDLE DUM, and DINAH struggle to swim in the ocean of tears.

TWEEDLE DEE: How do we make her stop?

TWEEDLE DUM: I don't know! She's a girl, a giant girl, and she's crying— So.. uh... Flowers? Chocolate?
TWEEDLE DEE: Chocolate got us into this mess, Dummy! We don't want that giant getting any bigger!

ALICE: I'm not a *giant*, I'm just a girl! And I want to go home! *(Loudly crying)* Waahhh!!

DINAH is hidden under the waving blue fabric as MOUSE, and several bird characters, DODO, CANARY, SONGBIRD, EAGLET, OWL, MAGPIE, and PARROT are pulled into the river of tears, trying desperately to swim.

DODO: What,what! Look lively gentle-birds we've been pulled into a squall!
CANARY: *(Up at ALICE)* What is that thing?
OWL: You mean WHHHOOOO—
MAGPIE: Whoever she is, she's getting my feathers all wet!
PARROT: *(Mimicking)* All wet!
ALICE wails.
EAGLET: Whatever shall we do, Dodo?!
DODO: Hard to Starboard! Full sails! Land Ho— and other nautical expressions!

MOUSE: At least I lost that horrible little cat!

DINAH bursts out of the fabric like she's bursting out of the water. MOUSE and BIRDS all shriek!

MOUSE & BIRDS: CAT!

48

DINAH: Yes! I'm a Cat! *(With a yowl)* And cats hate water! *(She starts to cry along with ALICE.)*

TWEEDLE DEE: Oh no! Not you too! No more tears!

SONGBIRD: Perhaps we should drink the tears! Nothing like a bit of salt water to clear the pipes! *(Gargling first, she starts to sing operatically)* LA LA LAAAAAAA!

TWEEDLE DUM: *(Shouting over the singing)* That's it! "Drink Me!"

TWEEDLE DEE: *(Automatically, trying to speak in his 1950's style while also treading water. To Audience)* Do you look down on all you meet? Does it make you sad, wallow, and weep? Would you like to be lighter? Brighter? ... Are your tears so big you could drown a mouse?

MOUSE: Yes!

ALICE: (Sniffling) Yes, I suppose so...

TWEEDLE DEE: Then try, "Drink me!" Just one sip will make you lighter than a feather, dancing on air... Like a fresh sweater out of the dryer ... you will literally shrink!

ALICE: Out of the what?

MOUSE: *(Shouting up to ALICE)* Just drink it already!

ALICE: Oh, alright.

(Slide whistle is heard going down, and ALICE is swept on to the stage next to DINAH center.)

DINAH: Miss Alice! You're small again!

ALICE: I don't know what good it's done me. We're still on the wrong side of the door, and now I'm likely to drown in my own tears!

CHESHIRE CAT 1 enters, backstroking through the water.

CHESHIRE CAT 1: Oh, I wouldn't worry about that.

ALICE: And why not?

CHESHIRE CAT1: Ever see water go down a drain?

ALICE: No?

CHESHIRE CAT 1: *(Backstroking off the stage, as the sound of water draining slowly begins to rise)* You're about to…

ALL: *(As if they were being pulled into a tidepool)* Waaaaaahhhhhhhhhh!!!!

Lights blackout as draining sound continues. After the drain empties, the music turns to Scene change. MUSIC abruptly halts and LIGHTS come back up on CHESHIRE CATS 2-9 sitting on a bench holding Alice in Wonderland programs.

CHESHIRE CAT 2: I don't get it? Did they get flushed down the toilet?

CHESHIRE CAT 3: Is it almost intermission? I have to pee!

CHESHIRE CAT 4: *(Turning over an empty popcorn tub)* I need more popcorn.

CHESHIRE CAT 5: *(Loud whisper)* You're not supposed to have that in here!

CHESHIRE CAT 6: No food or drink in the auditorium.

CHESHIRE CAT 7: There is a sign and everything.

CHESHIRE CAT 8 & 9: And no flash photography.

CHESHIRE CAT 2: Seriously? Did they get flushed down the toilet?

CHESHIRE CAT 3: Don't say toilet— I have to pee!

CHESHIRE CAT 5: *(Suddenly realizing)* I have to pee too!

CHESHIRE CAT 6: Me too!

CHESHIRE CAT 7, 8 & 9: So do we!

(CATS 3, and 5-9 start to fidget in their seats.)

CHESHIRE CAT 3: Don't say wee!

CHESHIRE CAT 5: Is it intermission yet??

CHESHIRE CAT 4: *(Looking at the program)* Yes. Yes, it is.

CATS look at audience. LIGHTS blackout.
Intermission.

ACT TWO

Scene 1

Curtain opens to a beautiful Wonderland garden, with long blades of grass six feet tall. Clocks and Playing cards hang from the ceiling. Upstage center there is a large tiered platform, painted like a chess board.

Beautiful music plays, Amilcare Ponchielli's "Dance of the Hours." Lovely dancing flowers begin a beautiful, but charmingly comical, dance. At every pause in the music, they pose at the audience and sigh at how lovely they are, what a beautiful day it is, etc. ROSE, LILY, CHRYSANTHEMUM, DAFFODIL, POPPY, VIOLET, AMARYLLIS, JASMINE, PETAL, MARIGOLD, IRIS, and DAISY are featured. The chorus is made up of smaller flowers: BABY'S BREATH, CARNATIONS, and FERNS.

Once the dance is over, we hear the end of the draining water. ALICE, DINAH, the TWEEDLES, MOUSE and BIRDS roll out onto the stage, out of the blue fabric, like they are being washed ashore. FLOWERS all squeal, running offstage to avoid the "water."

FLOWERS: *(FEATURED FLOWERS Variously, as they help other flowers exit)* Come along, dears!... Away from the water!... Watch your stems!... Don't let your roots get wet!.. Don't cry, Baby's Breath!... *(At the water/intruders)* What in carnation! How rude!

ALICE: *(Getting up)* However did we get here? We're in the garden! We made it!...But...how?

MOUSE: *(Sighing, and pushing up his large glasses)* It really is quite simple, the water and centrifugal force of the drain pushed us through the door. *(Laughing at her, and then to the audience)* Don't worry your little head about it, I wouldn't expect *a girl* like you to understand.

ALICE and DINAH both cross their arms.

ALICE: Oh really?

SONGBIRD: *(Shaking out her feathers)* Oh, don't mind him. He's just mouse-splaining.

MOUSE: I am not. If *you* understood the science, I wouldn't have to explain anything, birdbrain.

EAGLET: Oh, my feathers were not meant to be wet. *(At ALICE, snapping)* I'm not a duck you know!

ALICE: What are you then, may I ask?

DODO: Introductions! What, what!

BIRDS all line up.

CANARY: I am a Canary Bird, known for my sunny color and song.

EAGLET: I am an Eaglet, all soft and snowy, now. But one day, I'll be an eagle! Big, Bald, and Strong! *(He poses with strong arms.)*

OWL: I am the mother Owl. Both noble and wise.

MAGPIE: I am a Magpie. I collect shiny things, and fly over farms looking for pies. *(After a beat)* Pies on windowsills, that is.

SONGBIRD: I am a Songbird, I warble, and sing—

PARROT: *(Mimicking)* I am a Songbird, I warble, and sing—

SONGBIRD: He's a Parrot. He's annoying.

PARROT: Annoying!

DODO: And I am the one and only Dodo— What, what! *(Bowing)* Lord, liege, master, and other honorary titles!

ALICE: A Dodo! How wonderful!

DODO: Yes, I know. I am quite wonderful, aren't I?

MOUSE: *(After a beat)* I'm a Mouse. *(At Dinah)* But you know that already don't you, Cat?!

ALICE: Now, now— she's just a kitten. She can't help that she wants to chase you. It's just her nature. AND her name is Dinah.

DINAH: Yeah! And you run funny too!

MOUSE: Do not!

DINAH: Do too!

Stepping between MOUSE and DINAH, ALICE draws their attention to TWEEDLE DEE and TWEEDLE DUM.

ALICE: And who are you fine gentlemen?

TWEEDLES strike a pose.

TWEEDLE DEE: He's Tweedle Dum.

TWEEDLE DUM: And *I'm* Tweedle Dee.

TWEEDLE DEE: *(Sighing and coming out of the pose)* No! You're supposed to say "He's Tweedle Dee" You're Tweedle Dum, Dummy!

TWEEDLE DUM: I can't say "*You're* Tweedle Dum," *I'm* Tweedle Dum!

TWEEDLE DEE: I didn't say, say "You're Tweedle Dum," I said, say " He's Tweedle Dee!"

TWEEDLE DUM: *(Takes a big breath to fight, and then stops, confused)* Wait...I'm confused... what am I supposed to say again?

TWEEDLE DEE: Forget it! *(Turning back to ALICE, annoyed)* I'm Tweedle Dee. This is my brother.

TWEEDLE DUM: Tweedle Dum!

TWEEDLE DEE: Yeah, he's the dumb one alright.

ALICE: Well, it's a pleasure to meet you both. I thank you for your help. Without, the river of tears, and the *(looking at MOUSE)* centrifugal force? *(Back to TWEEDLES)* we never would have made it into this beautiful garden!

TWEEDLE DEE: No problem! It was our pleasure.

TWEEDLE DUM: *(Still confused)* What she say about a horse?

TWEEDLE DEE: She says you're as dumb as a horse's behind!

ALICE: No, no— I would never—

MAGPIE: *(Stepping in)* And what kind of bird are you?

CANARY: Your wings are not very long— *(To the others)* she must be flightless.

EAGLET: No feathers, either.

OWL: Are you molting, sweetheart?

SONGBIRD: Can you sing?

ALICE: *(Laughing)* No, no, I'm not a bird. I'm just a girl.

FLOWERS re-enter finding their places again. DAFFODIL and other featured flowers interrupt ALICE, pushing through the group and lining up downstage center. BIRDS, MOUSE, TWEEDLES, and DINAH push to SR and SL, leaving ALICE center with the flowers.

ALICE: Look at all the flowers! Oh, they're so beautiful!

DAFFODIL: You better do more than look, honey. You're standing in my spot.

ROSE: Positions, ladies! Positions!

ALICE: Oh my! They talk!

AMARYLLIS: Of course, we talk!

PETAL: If there is anyone worth talking to—

CHRYSANTHEMUM: *(To PETAL next to her)* Or about!

CHRYSANTHEMUM and PETAL laugh.

POPPY: We dance too.

VIOLET: What did you think we do?

LILY: Just stand here in a row and look pretty?

ALICE: Well… yes. That's what flowers do where I am from.

IRIS: And what kind of garden do you come from then?

ALICE: I don't come from a garden.

MARIGOLD: Do you suppose she's a wildflower?

JASMINE: *(Disgusted)* She smells wild.

DAISY: Looks it too.

PETAL: You can tell she hasn't slept in a proper bed for weeks.

CHRYSANTHEMUM and PETAL give a snooty, "Hunh."

ALICE: *(Getting mad)* Excuse me—

ROSE: *(Stepping in)* Just what species, or genus, are you, dear?

DAISY cuts in. Then the rest of the flowers are quick— one right after the other:

DAISY: I'm a Bellis Perrenis— a Daisy—

MARIGOLD: Marigold—

AMARYLLIS: Amaryllis—

DAFFODIL: Daffodil—

IRIS: Iris—

POPPY: Poppy—

VIOLET: Violet—

LILY: Lily—

JASMINE: Jasmine—

CHRYSANTHEMUM: Chrysanthemum—

PETAL: I'm a Ranunculus asiaticus— but you can call me Petal.

(After a beat)

ROSE: And I am a Rose, by any other name… *(To ALICE)* And you are?

60

ALICE: Well, I suppose I am a Genus— Human-us — an Alice.

(ALL Flowers begin to gossip and whisper amongst themselves, featured flowers look her up and down disapprovingly.)

DAISY: *(To IRIS)* Have you ever heard of an Alice that looked like that?

IRIS: Come to think of it, have you ever heard of an Alice?

DAFFODIL: Her blossom is wilting—

POPPY: Her petals are too pale—

VIOLET: *(Pointing at ALICE's knees)* Look at her stems! The way they bend in the middle— it's revolting!

FLOWERS: *(Variously)* Uhg!...Ooh!... Gasp!

AMARYLLIS: *(Grabbing ALICE's hands)* And her leaves have split ends— did you see that?

FLOWERS: *(Louder, Variously)* Uhg!...Ooh!... Gasp!

JASMINE: And no fragrance at all!

LILLY: What an odd flower, an Alice?

DINAH: *(Butting in)* But she's not a flower!

CHRYSANTHEMUM: Not a flower! *(Aside to PETAL next to her)* I know what she is...

PETAL nods knowingly. CHRYSANTHEMUM and PETAL laugh.

CHRYSANTHEMUM & PETAL: She's a weed!

FLOWERS: *(Loudest, Variously)* Uhg!...Ooh!... Gasp!

ALICE: I am not a weed!

AMARYLLIS: Well, you wouldn't expect her to admit it now would you?

IRIS: No, you wouldn't.

FLOWERS all shake their heads knowingly.

PETAL: I suspected it all along!

DAISY: Nothing more than a weed!

ALICE: *(Very mad now)* I am not a weed! I am a girl! Just a girl! And if I were my right size, I could pick each and every one of you! *(FLOWERS gasp)* I could pluck the petals from your heads, one by one! *(FLOWERS gasp louder)* I— I— I could cut the blossoms from your stems and make myself a crown!

FLOWERS all grasp their throats, terrified! BABY'S BREATH start to cry... The WHITE QUEEN enters in behind ALICE. The WHITE QUEEN strongly resembles the chess piece that bears her name, dressed all in white with a conical skirt that reaches the floor, and tall white crown that puts her head at a point. She is kind and commanding, everything a Queen should be. She reminds Alice of her big sister Ada.

WHITE QUEEN: Really, my dear, you are making the Baby's breath cry.

BABY'S BREATH cry dramatically.

ROSE: *(Bowing)* Your majesty!

ALL except ALICE and DINAH bow.

ALICE: *(Bowing a beat after the others)* Your majesty— I'm sorry— I was just so angry— They called me—

WHITE QUEEN: Rule #52, dear: Never place blame, but forgive with impunity.

ALICE: Forgive? I suppose I could do that…*(Still mad)*… I forgive you for calling me a weed, and I am sorry if I threatened to turn you all into a bouquet.

FLOWERS all gasp again.

PETAL: *(Loud whisper to CHRYSANTHEMUM)* The idea!

CHRYSANTHEMUM: She's definitely a weed!

ALICE: Yes, thank you so very much for gracing me with your presence and teaching me all about flowers. Thanks a whole BUNCH!

FLOWERS gasp, even louder.

MARIGOLD: Did she say bunch?!

ALICE: *(With a sly smile)* And to think I made a whole Daisy chain just this morning…

FLOWERS gasp, the loudest. DAISY faints into another flowers arms.

WHITE QUEEN: Perhaps that is enough forgiveness. You may leave us.

MARIGOLD: *(Gasps)* Did she say leaves?

WHITE QUEEN: You may go.

ALL exit, except DINAH who joins ALICE and the WHITE QUEEN center stage.

Scene 2

Scene 2 continues from Scene 1 without a blackout.

WHITE QUEEN: *(To DINAH)* And you are?

DINAH: I'm her cat.

WHITE QUEEN: Then you may stay.

ALICE: My name is—

WHITE QUEEN: Alice, of course, I know who you are. Queen Alice—

ALICE: But I'm not—

WHITE QUEEN: Rule # 37— A Queen never interrupts.

ALICE: But I'm *not*—

WHITE QUEEN: Rule #38, dear— A Queen is never not agreeable.

ALICE: But I'm not—

WHITE QUEEN Don't forget Rule #39—A Queen never repeats.

ALICE: But I'm not a Queen!

WHITE QUEEN: Of course you aren't, not yet, you're just a girl.

ALICE: That's what I keep telling everyone.

ALICE and WHITE QUEEN walk together SR, with DINAH following just behind. When they reach SR, they turn to SL, and back again, slowly, like they are enjoying a stroll.

WHITE QUEEN: But this is *your* world Alice. Don't you remember? "In my world, there are no husbands, or wives but Kings and Queens—"

ALICE: But there can only be one Queen at a time, right? I know that from my history lessons.

WHITE QUEEN: "And no lessons, just games. Never-ending games of cards, and chess, and croquet—" You see, I'm the White Queen. One might say the most important piece in the game of Chess.

ALICE: You mean you're a chess piece? What nonsense!

WHITE QUEEN: "Yes! Utter nonsense! *(Taking Dinah by the hand, and beginning to dance with her)* And all the animals, the trees, and the flowers, will walk, and talk, and dance— especially dance! And wear gloves, of course. That's only good manners, Dinah.

DINAH: *(Laughing at the dancing)* Yes, your majesty.

ALICE:*(After a beat)* If you're the White Queen, does that mean there is another queen of some other color?

WHITE QUEEN: Oh, there are many queens— the Queen of Diamonds, of Clubs, of Spades— But they're card Queens, much more *common* than a chess piece like myself.

ALICE: I suppose there are hundreds of cards out there, and just two queens a chess set.

WHITE QUEEN: Yes, but then I must remind myself of Rule #62. A Queen is as much below as she is above the commoners, for they know tricks that she does not.

ALICE: Yes, I imagine cards do know all kinds of tricks.

WHITE QUEEN: *(She finds this slightly distasteful)* Yes. Chess is more of a game of strategy, wouldn't you say? It takes a lot more than tricks to win over the Red Queen, I'll tell you that.

ALICE: Is she the other chess Queen?

WHITE QUEEN: Yes. But I'm afraid her temper is as red as her dress. If it were up to her she would be the *only* Queen in Wonderland. Let her know that you're *the* Queen Alice and it will be "off with your head" before you can turn it.

ALICE: But I'm not *the* Queen Alice, am I? I can't be. I'm—

WHITE QUEEN: Just a girl, I know. But I told you, dear. It's *your* world.

ALICE: Does that mean this is my dream? That you and everyone else in Wonderland are...not real ?

WHITE QUEEN: Perhaps we are a dream... But what makes a dream world any less real?

FROM offstage we hear the chattering sounds of the card Queens and the mother CUCKOO bird.

CUCKOO: *(Offstage)* Serpent! Serpent!

WHITE QUEEN: Oh no, it's the card Queens and that dithering Cuckoo bird. I must go, dear Alice. I do not want to appear rude, so it's best that I do not appear at all. *(Calling offstage)* Yoohoo! White Knight!

WHITE KNIGHT: *(Gallops on to escort her.)* I am here, my Queen. To the rescue!

WHITE QUEEN: That's very kind of you, thank you. Now take me away!

ALICE: Wait— You said that I would become Queen Alice. But how will I do that?

WHITE QUEEN: Checkmate, of course!

CUCKOO: *(Louder, but still offstage)* Serpent! Serpent!

WHITE QUEEN: I really must dash! Goodbye Alice! Goodbye Dinah! *(She exits with the WHITE KNIGHT.)*

DINAH: Goodbye!

The card Queens, Queen of DIAMOND, CLUBS and SPADES enter, each rock and bounce babies with long white swaddling blankets. On the blankets are the Ace symbols for their suit (i.e. A♠, A♣, & A♦) After them, comes the CUCKOO bird. She is a strange and rattled bird pushing a nest on wheels with one very large egg in it, like a stroller.

SPADES: Honestly, it was a tree root, not a serpent.

CLUBS: *(Aside to SPADES)* She really is Cuckoo, isn't she?

SPADES and CLUBS giggle quietly at her joke.

CUCKOO: *(Not hearing CLUBS)* As if it wasn't trouble enough laying eggs, I've got to be on the lookout for serpents day and night. I haven't had a wink of sleep in three weeks. I tell you, I'm this close to sneaking my egg into another bird's nest. A Nanny-bird, that's what I need!

Meeting the Queens and Cuckoo center, ALICE steps forward with DINAH just behind. During the following, CUCKOO turns away from the group and stays on the lookout, cocking her head from side to side, twitching back and forth, looking for Serpents, everywhere but at ALICE and DINAH.

68

ALICE: Good afternoon, your majesties.

DIAMONDS: Is it afternoon already?

SPADES: Don't pay any attention to us, dear. The only time we find, is when our children are asleep.

CLUBS: Sleep? My child does not sleep! I simply don't allow it. I yell in his ears, if he even starts to snore. It's the only way to raise an alert child.

ALICE: That's terrible!

CLUBS: That's motherhood.

Queens all nod in agreement.

SPADES: But you don't want him *too* alert. Whenever he seems just a little *too* bright-eyed I put a bag over his head. It's the only way to raise a calm child.

ALICE: But that can't be right.

CLUBS: She's just being a good mother.

Queens all nod in agreement.

DIAMONDS: As for me, I strictly adhere to the old lullaby: Speak roughly to your little boy and beat him when he sneezes, He only does it to annoy, because he knows it teases!

ALL QUEENS: *(They bounce their babies on each wah)* Wah! Wah! Wah!

ALICE: Now, that's really terrible!

CLUBS: That's only the first verse.

DIAMONDS: I speak severely to my boy, I beat him when he sneezes, For he can thoroughly enjoy the pepper when he pleases!

ALL QUEENS: *(They bounce their babies on each wah)* Wah! Wah! Wah!

Queens nod in agreement once more.

ALICE: What?! That's horrible.

CLUBS: That's good sense.

DIAMONDS: What do you do when your little boy sneezes?

ALICE: I don't have a little boy, but if I did I'd say "Gesundheit."

SPADES: What kind of gibberish is that?

DIAMONDS: Seems to me if everybody minded their business the world would go around a deal faster than it does.

Queens all nod in agreement, giving nasty looks to ALICE.

CLUBS: *(Changing the subject after a beat)* Well, there is one thing we all agree on with our little boys. Am I right, ladies?

Queens smile in anticipation of the old joke—cuddling their baby boys close in a sickeningly sweet fashion they say together—

ALL QUEENS: They're "one of a kind!"

Small child dressed as TWO of DIAMONDS comes running by screaming at the top of his lungs. He faces the audience, screams again, then circling ALICE, he runs offstage. Queens ignore it.

DIAMONDS: *(To ALICE and DINAH)* Ignore him. He's a terrible two.

CUCKOO *finally turns around and notices ALICE, then*
immediately mistakes her for a serpent.

CUCKOO: *(Pointing at ALICE)* Serpent! Serpent!

ALICE: I am not a serpent! *(To Audience, exhausted)* Why
does everyone think I'm something here?

CUCKOO: Serpent!

ALICE: I am not a serpent. I'm just a little girl.

CUCKOO: A likely story indeed! I've seen a good many little
girls in my time, but never one with a neck such as that!

ALICE: What's wrong with my neck?

CUCKOO: You're a serpent! There's no use denying it! Next,
you're going to tell me you've never ate an egg before!

ALICE: Well, of course I've ate an egg before—

CUCKOO: Serpent!

ALICE: You must know that little girls eat eggs as much as
serpents do.

CUCKOO: Then little girls are serpents too!

ALICE: That makes no sense!

ALL QUEENS: *(Bounce their babies as they sing)* Wah! Wah!
Wah!

During the following, the TWO of DIAMONDS comes running
back in, circling them until he ends up behind DINAH. By the
time she finishes her line he has a hold of her tail, and yanks!

ALICE: *(Turning to DINAH)* I'm starting to understand why the
White Queen left...

DINAH: I don't know the babies are cute at least, *(laughing)* and that bird is out of her—*(yank)* YOOOWWWLLLL!

TWO of DIAMONDS runs off again.

CUCKOO: What was that?!
ALICE: That naughty number two came up behind her and pulled her tail!
CUCKOO: Tail?! Is she a serpent?!
ALICE: No, for goodness sake! She's a cat!

QUEENS all gasp. CUCKOO freezes. Just as she freezes we hear the first few notes of the Can Can from "Orpheus in the Underworld" by Jacques Offenbach.

CUCKOO: Did you say—

DINAH steps out from behind ALICE revealing her tail and ears. CUCKOO takes a big breath and screams!

CUCKOO: CAAAAATTTT!! *(Clutching her egg to her chest while pulling a comically large wooden club from her nest stroller, she brandishes it at DINAH)* Away from my baby, CAT!
DINAH: Uh-oh.

DINAH dashes offstage with the CUCKOO bird on her tail, as the music gets into full swing. Now the cat is the one to be chased! ALICE follows, trying to save her poor cat from the CUCKOO bird. QUEENS follow as well, not to miss out on any of the action.

The following montage is the climax of Wonderland zaniness to the music of the Can Can:

DINAH runs from the CUCKOO BIRD, with ALICE just behind.
The TWO of DIAMONDS runs from his mother the QUEEN of DIAMONDS.
WHITE QUEEN enters in a dash with two QUEENS running after her to talk, they smile and wave animatedly.
FROG FOOTMAN skips quickly across, still holding his giant envelope.
MOUSE returns with DINAH chasing after him, and then ALICE runs across with the CUCKOO bird now chasing her!

Twenty or so beats into the song, a line of FLOWERS enter doing an elaborate Can Can dance.

Now, as a line of flowers exits, the TWEEDLES, DODO, CANARY, MAGPIE, OWL, PARROT and SONGBIRD hilariously attempt the Can Can. Flowers shortly return overtaking them as they exit.

MOUSE runs across with DINAH running just behind, but she is not chasing mouse for the CUCKOO bird is hot on her tail. ALICE runs just a beat behind.

Rolling platform with the, as yet unseen, MAD HATTER's Tea Party, rolls across. MAD HATTER sits center of the table in a large glorious chair. MARCH HARE sits to the right of him.

WHITE QUEEN meets the WHITE KNIGHT "riding" centerstage, he looks to see who is after her. CUCKOO enters brandishing her club, WHITE KNIGHT "gallops" away with the WHITE QUEEN just behind her. CUCKOO follows.

THEN, in the last 30 seconds they do it all again! As FAST AS THEY CAN!

FLOWERS once again retake the stage dancing the Can Can.

MOUSE runs across with DINAH just behind, but now the CUCKOO bird is being chased by the TWO of DIAMONDS, who has stolen her enormous wooden club.

QUEEN Of DIAMONDS, and the two other queens follow just behind. This times with the whole CARD deck running in behind them in a procession.

TWEEDLES and the BIRDS dance with the FLOWERS.

This time though, instead of the MAD HATTER's Tea Party, the CATERPILLAR, is rolled in on her mushroom toadstool, hitting SL as the music ends.

AT THE SAME TIME, just as the music is ending, ALICE wanders in, bewildered, lost, and looking for DINAH. A beat after the music has ended, and everyone is in a wonderful pose, she backs up and over the CUCKOO's nest. And, once

again, she is on her back with her feet in the air, and her
ridiculous bloomers on display. Everyone remains frozen in
their pose, ALICE rights herself up, and sighs.

ALICE: I've really gone over the Cuckoo's nest, haven't I?
PARROT: *(Unfreezing, flaps his wings and shouts)* Crackers!

ALL exit except ALICE and the CATERPILLAR.

Scene 3

Scene 3 continues from Scene 2 without a blackout.

A Note on the CATERPILLAR: The Caterpillar is one part actor, one part set piece, and one part group. The main actor sits on top of her mushroom seat, while three more actors stand behind her or the set piece with their arms through holes, acting as the caterpillar's other limbs. The three behind-the-set actors will be wearing different colored gloves: GREEN, RED, and BLUE. The main actor wears black gloves.

Where many Alice in Wonderland caterpillars are comical, furious, or just a little bit strange— Ours is a little more elegant, with her satin arm length gloves, large goggle sunglasses, and long cigarette holder. Think Holly Golightly from Breakfast at Tiffany's. Only— you know, a bug.

CATERPILLAR: *(Coolly)* Who are you?
ALICE: *(Getting up)* I'm afraid I can't answer that with much certainty. I've been mistaken for so many things today already, a giant, a bird, a flower, and a serpent. I'm really just a girl. *(With a sniff)* And I've lost my cat.
CATERPILLAR: Who—
ALICE: Her name is Dinah. She's just a kitten, but no one really seems to like her down here.
CATERPILLAR: — are you?
ALICE: What?

CATERPILLAR: Not what. Who? Are? You?

ALICE: I'm just a girl, I just said— Oh, this is so frustrating. I've been as small as a mouse, and as big as a house, and small all over again. I've been so many sizes— *(Finally really, looking at her, ALICE realizes she's talking to a CATERPILLAR)* Oh— oh my! You're a Caterpillar!

GREEN, RED, and BLUE hands open and shut in a ripple.

CATERPILLAR: Yes. I am the Caterpillar.

ALICE: Well, one day you will understand what it's like... first, you're just a caterpillar, and then *woosh!* You're a big beautiful butterfly...*(Looking at the size of her)* Very big, I imagine.

CATERPILLAR: Just?

GREEN, RED, and BLUE hands open and shut in a ripple, again.

ALICE: What?

CATERPILLAR: I am not *just* a caterpillar.

ALICE: Then, who are you?

CATERPILLAR: Who? Are? You?

ALICE: Didn't I *just* say that?

CATERPILLAR: Just, just, just... Just a caterpillar. Just a girl. Did you know that a caterpillar will shed her skin four or five times before she becomes a butterfly? That she has twelve eyes to see you with? Can eat a thousand times her own weight? Did you know that some caterpillars are poisonous? That they can spin silk?

ALICE: *(Nervous)* Are you... poisonous?

CATERPILLAR: Are you?

ALICE: *(Sigh)* This is getting us nowhere.

CATERPILLAR: Where would you like to go?

ALICE: Oh, I don't much care where— as long as it's somewhere.

CATERPILLAR: Oh, you're sure to do that... if only you walk long enough.

ALICE: That's what the cat said. Let me guess... some caterpillars can tell the future?

CATERPILLAR: No. That's just common sense. Everywhere is somewhere. It is *you* that makes it *your* destination. You just have to decide.

ALICE: Decide?

CATERPILLAR: Do you go left *(GREEN points stage right)* to the White Queen, the flowers, and a door you've already been through? Or right *(RED points stage left)* to a party, a game, and... the Red Queen?

ALICE: I've heard about her... is she as ill tempered as they say?

GLOVES make corresponding gestures with their colors.

CATERPILLAR: Some girls get the blues, some are green with envy... others get the mean reds...

ALICE: The mean reds?

CATERPILLAR: It's a feeling. Like you're afraid, and you don't know why...

ALICE: I think... I want... I think I just want to find my cat!

CATERPILLAR: ...Just...

ALICE: *(Losing her temper)* Have you seen her? She's a kitten. Black with a white apron? Pink bow?

CATERPILLAR: Yes, she went that way. *(BLUE points stage left.)*

ALICE: Thank you. That's all I wanted to know. *(Starts to exit.)*

CATERPILLAR: What size do you want to be?

ALICE: What do you mean?

CATERPILLAR: "As small as a mouse, as big as a house, and small again—" what size do you want to be?

ALICE: The normal size, I suppose.

CATERPILLAR: One side makes you taller, the other makes you smaller.

ALICE: The other side of what?

CATERPILLAR: My mushroom, of course. Take some with you if you like.

ALICE: *(Taking some of the mushroom)* ...Thank you. My name is Alice, by the way.

ALICE starts to go Stage Left crossing the CATERPILLAR.

CATERPILLAR: Alice... *(ALICE stops and turns back to her)* if a little caterpillar can shed her skin, hold a thousand times her own weight, spin silk, and become a butterfly... just what do you think a girl can do?

LIGHTS blackout for scene change.

Scene 4

LIGHTS come up on the MAD HATTER's tea party. It's a long table with the MAD HATTER sitting center in a tall-back chair, like a throne. MARCH HARE sits Stage right of the MAD HATTER, and the MOUSE sits far stage left. A tiny DORMOUSE sits between the MAD HATTER and the MOUSE. She and the MOUSE are both sleeping.

A NOTE on the SET: While it looks like there are several chairs on either side of the HATTER's chair, it should actually be two long benches with several chair backs attached. This allows for characters to slide up and down the length of the table without difficulty.

ALICE enters from SR, approaching the table. Before she can speak, MAD HATTER shouts at her!

MAD HATTER: No room! No room! No room! You can't sit down!
ALICE: *(Laughing)* What do you mean no room? There are plenty of seats.

CHESHIRE CAT 1 pops out from behind the MAD HATTER's chair. He lounges across the top. No one seems to notice. They are too busy with their tea.

ALICE: You!
CHESHIRE CAT 1: Yes, it's me.

ALICE: Where are the rest of your nine?

CHESHIRE CAT 1: Off having lives of their own, of course. Have you made an introduction yet?

ALICE: *(Whispering)* They say there is no room.

CHESHIRE CAT 1: They always say that. *(Gesturing at him)* He's a March Hare, and he's a Hatter. They're both mad.

ALICE: Perhaps, since it's July, and no longer spring—you know, *(she whispers) mating season...* Maybe, the March Hare is not so mad?

CHESHIRE CAT 1: Oh, but he is an amorous rabbit. No doubt he'll be just mad about you the moment he sees you.

MARCH HARE: *(He sees her, then dramatically slides down the bench to be near her)* Heelllo—who is this?

CHESHIRE CAT 1: See?

MARCH HARE: Have a seat right here by me... whatever you name is.

MAD HATTER: No room, no room, no room!

MARCH HARE: *(Never looking away from ALICE)* Nonsense! There is plenty of room, right here next to me.

ALICE sits in a chair at the end of the table. One away from the MARCH HARE.

ALICE: Uh— thank you. My name is Alice.

MARCH HARE: *(Still staring)* What a lovely name, Alice. Have some wine.

ALICE: *(Looking at the table)* I don't see any wine.

MAD HATTER: There isn't any.

ALICE: It wasn't very polite of you to offer wine if you don't have any wine.

MAD HATTER: It wasn't very polite of you to sit down where you weren't invited. Especially without any wine. Don't you know to bring wine to a party?

ALICE: Is this a party? You're such a small group at such a large table, and half of you are asleep.

MOUSE: *(Jolting awake)* I'm not asleep. I heard everything you fellows were saying. *(He sees it's ALICE)* You! You and you're terrible cat have run me ragged. I can barely keep my eyes open— and you smudged my glasses!

ALICE: Dinah?! Have you seen her?

MAD HATTER: *(Squinting at ALICE)* Your hair needs cutting. It's much too long.

MARCH HARE: *(Never looking away from ALICE)* Nonsense! She has beautiful hair. I'm a pretty nice hare too, if you didn't notice.

ALICE: *(Ignoring MARCH HARE)* You should learn not to make such personal remarks. It's rude.

MAD HATTER: Hmmm… That's interesting. Tell me this. Why is a raven like a writing desk?

ALICE: *(Suddenly recognizing him, she laughs)* I know you! You're the one in the shower!

MAD HATTER: Now who's getting personal.

ALICE: I mean, I am very sorry about that... But you were right! The door behind the curtain is the one that brought me here. Of course, I had to drink a potion to get smaller. And then a cake to get taller. Then I got really upset and cried a whole river of tears. Then I got smaller again— and then *whoosh!* I went right through the door.

MAD HATTER: Nonsense! Utter nonsense! Wouldn't you say, March Hare?

MARCH HARE: Yes, utter nonsense!

MOUSE: What do you expect? She's just a girl, after all.

MARCH HARE: But she is sure pretty, isn't she?

ALICE: It is not nonsense! That is exactly how it happened! *(To MAD HATTER)* You were there! *(To MOUSE)* And you! And... Dinah! Where is Dinah? Have you seen her?

MOUSE: Seen her? Everywhere I go, there she is! Chasing me this way, chasing me that way! You're cat—

DORMOUSE: *(Startling awake, she sings)* Twinkle, twinkle little bat, How I wonder where you're at. Up above the world you fly, like a tea-tray in the sky— *(over and over, then falling back asleep)* Twinkle, twinkle, twinkle, twinkle, twinkle, twinkle —

CHESHIRE CAT 1: Someone nudge her, she's off the record...

MOUSE nudges DORMOUSE and she settles back into a gentle snore.

ALICE: She is a sleepy little thing isn't she?

MOUSE: *(Cleaning his glasses)* Actually, she's a Dormouse. Which isn't a mouse at all. She's more of a squirrel. Dormouse comes from the latin "dormeus" which means "sleepy one." This is because the Dormouse is most known for their long bouts of hibernation. In fact, the Romans used to eat them as a cure for sleeplessness.

DORMOUSE: *(Wakes up screaming, jumping up from her seat, her words run into each other in one long screech)*

86

ROMAANNNSSSS!!! NO-NOT-THE-ROMANS-WHEN-IN-ROME-
DON'T-DO-AS-THE-ROMANS-DO-NO-NO-NO! *(And back asleep, she sits with a gentle snore.)*
ALICE: Oh my, I hope she doesn't do that again. Best not to say the R-word anymore
Quickly, one right after the other.
MAD HATTER: What? Raven?
ALICE: No—
MARCH HARE: Radiant?
ALICE: No—
MAD HATTER: Room?
ALICE: No—
MARCH HARE: Remarkable?
ALICE: No—
MAD HATTER: Reasonable?
ALICE: NO!
MOUSE: *(After a beat)* What? Romans?
DORMOUSE: *(Wakes up screaming, jumping up, her words run into each other in one long screech)*ROMAANSS!NO-NOT-THE-ROMANS-WHEN-IN-ROME-DON'T-DO-AS-THE-ROMANS-DO-NO-NO-NO! *(And back asleep, with a gentle snore.)*
ALICE: Please... don't say it again...

MAD HATTER: What day of the month is it?
ALICE: I'm not sure, the twentieth?

MAD HATTER: *(Taking out a large pocket watch and looking at it)* Two days off! I told you butter would not fix it.

MARCH HARE: But it was the best butter—

MAD HATTER: You put butter in your pocket watch? No wonder it's broken.

MARCH HARE: It was the *best* butter—

MAD HATTER: You shouldn't have used the butter knife, it must have got some crumbs in it. Next it'll be telling us it's last week, when it's really tomorrow.

ALICE: What a funny watch— it tells you what day of the month it is, but not the o'clock!

MAD HATTER: Why should it? Does your watch tell you what *year* it is?

ALICE: Of course not— BUT that is because it stays the same year for such a long time.

MAD HATTER: Hmph. Have you guessed the riddle yet?

ALICE: Why is a Raven like a writing desk?

MAD HATTER: Yes?

ALICE: No— How is a Raven like a writing desk?

MAD HATTER: I haven't the slightest idea.

MOUSE: Nor I.

MARCH HARE: Not a clue.

ALICE: *(Sighing)* I think you might do something better with the time than waste it with riddles that have no answers.

MAD HATTER: If you knew Time as well as I do, you wouldn't talk about wasting *it*. It's him.

CHESHIRE CAT 1: He's right, you know. Great guy, loves to laugh.

MAD HATTER: Not anymore, not with me!

CHESHIRE CAT 1: Oh, really? Did you quarrel?

MAD HATTER: It was last March, just as he *(pointing at MARCH HARE)* went mad. I was singing at a concert for the Red Queen, one of my preferred arias— *(MAD HATTER opens his mouth to sing but he is interrupted by DORMOUSE.)*

DORMOUSE: *(Startling awake, she sings)* Twinkle, twinkle little bat, How I wonder where you're at. Up above the world you fly, like a tea-tray in the sky— *(over and over, then falling back asleep)* Twinkle, twinkle, twinkle, twinkle, twinkle, twinkle —

MOUSE nudges DORMOUSE and she settles back into a gentle snore.

MAD HATTER: Yes, well, I'd hardly finished the first verse when the Queen jumped up and bawled out, "He's murdering the time! Off with his head!"

ALICE: How dreadfully savage!

MAD HATTER: And ever since he won't do a thing I ask! Won't move forward, won't move back, he's simply implacable!

MARCH HARE: *(Sighing)* Immoveable…

DORMOUSE: *(Startles awake)* Stuck. *(Back to sleep.)*

MAD HATTER: And now it's always tea time.

ALICE: Oh, is that why there are so many place settings?

MADHATTER: *(Looks down at his tea then shouts)* CHANGE PLACES!

MARCH HARE and MADHATTER: *(Over and over, during the following action)* Move down! Move down! Move down!

MARCH HARE grabs ALICE pulling her to the bench and together they slide down, as MAD HATTER slides down the second bench, knocking DORMOUSE to the ground. MOUSE begrudgingly gets up and moves down to the opposite end of the table. DORMOUSE pulls herself up to the end seat, then goes back to sleep.

MAD HATTER: Without the time to clean up we just move down, over and over.
MARCH HARE: Around and around.
DORMOUSE: *(Awake)* It's exhausting. *(Asleep.)*

MOUSE: How irrational… Time is only a construct of society. Logically, tea time is not actually a set time at all. Tea time is —

DINAH enters from SL, poses in her pouncing style, she points at MOUSE.

DINAH: MOUSE!
MOUSE: *(Leaping up from his seat)* CAT! AHHHHH!!!!

DINAH chases him off SR.

ALICE: *(Getting up from the bench)* Oh no! Dinah! Dinah, would you please stop chasing that poor Mouse?! *(Sighing, she sits back down.)* Gone again.

DORMOUSE: *(Awake)* So exhausting. *(Asleep.)*

ALICE: My thoughts exactly.

WHITE RABBIT enters from SR.

WHITE RABBIT: There you are, Alice! I have been looking all over for you! You weren't at the Caucus-race, not with little Bill the lizard— you simply skipped the Pig and the Pepper! *(Turning to CHESHIRE CAT)* I thought you were going to keep her on book! And did I see the Mouse running from here? He's not even in this chapter!

CHESHIRE CAT 1: I don't know what you're talking about Rabbit. She's at the party, isn't she?

WHIT E RABBIT: Yes, I suppose, but we really must be going. Come along, Alice. We're very late.

ALICE: The White Rabbit! You're the reason I'm here! I was following you!

WHITE RABBIT: Yes, yes. *(To the party)* Not very quick is she?

MARCH HARE: But *so* pretty!

WHITE RABBIT: *(Speaking slowly, as if she is dumb.)* Ye-e-e-s, I'm the White Rabbit. Now follow me, the queen is waiting.

ALICE: Not the Red Queen?

WHITE RABBIT: *(Pulling her up out of her chair and towards SL exit)* Yes! You know who the Red Queen is, wonderful!

We're ahead of schedule. Now come along, dear! Tell me, do you play croquet?

WHITE RABBIT pushes ALICE off SL as lights blackout for scene change.

Scene 5

LIGHTS come up on four "rose bushes." These bushes are just like our flowers from the top of the act, only now they are grouped tightly together into four groups. The first group is made up of entirely Red Roses. The second and third group are mixed, both Red and White Roses, with a few that are in between with both Red and White petals. The fourth is an entirely White Rose bush.

There are four cards busily attempting to paint the white roses red: the SEVEN of SPADES, the EIGHT of DIAMONDS, the NINE of DIAMONDS, and the TEN of CLUBS.

EIGHT: Look out now, Nine! Don't go splashing paint all over me like that.

NINE: *(Sulking)* I can't help it, Seven jogged my elbow.

SEVEN: That's right, Nine. Always lay the blame on others!

TEN: You best be quiet Seven, I heard the Queen say only yesterday that *you* should be beheaded.

They all shudder, and pull at their collars. Then go back to painting.

WHITE/RED ROSE 1: *(With a giggle)* That tickles!

SEVEN: Quiet you! This is all your fault!

NINE: Yeah, you were supposed to be *RED* Roses!

WHITE ROSE 1: We can't help it.

WHITE ROSE 2: We were planted that way!

ALL ROSES: *(Variously)* Yes!..We can't help it!...It's not our fault!

TEN: Quiet down! Or I'll get the pruning shears! Then we'll all get beheaded.

ROSES gasp and quiet instantly.

EIGHT: That's more like it.

CARDS go back to painting as WHITE RABBIT and ALICE enter SR.

WHITE RABBIT: *(To CARDS)* What are you doing?!

CARDS startle, NINE throws his paint brush in the air, SEVEN and EIGHT run into one another, somehow they line up at attention.

NINE: Sir, it was the gardeners, you see. They accidentally planted—

WHITE RABBIT: Wait! *(CARDS freeze)* I simply don't have time for this! Alice, wait right here while I go see where the croquet will be played. *(He exits SL.)*

ALICE: Why are you painting those roses red?

CARDS unfreeze.

TEN: You see, Miss. The fact is, we were supposed to plant red roses.

NINE: For the *RED* Queen.

SEVEN: She loves red!

EIGHT: She wants everything red!

TEN: But we accidentally planted white roses.

NINE: So now we're painting them red.

SEVEN: So the Red Queen doesn't *see* red.

EIGHT: So we don't end up—

CARDS: Dead.

ALICE: Oh, I imagine it's worse because they are white. Because the White Queen is her nemesis.

TEN: Oh no!

NINE: We didn't even think of that!

SEVEN: Oh no!

EIGHT: Get back to work!

CARDS: Back to work!!

CARDS scramble back to painting the roses.

RED ROOK 1: *(From Offstage)* Make way for the Queen!

RED ROOK 2: *(From Offstage)* Make way for the Queen!

CARDS: *(Slapstick-running into one another, they throw themselves on the ground face first, saying variously)* The Queen!...The Queen!.... The Queen!

MUSIC starts "Carmen" by Georges Bizet and from SL comes a great procession Groups enters, parade from SL to SR, then circle around upstage to find their place:

Four red pawns as GUARDS.

CHILD CARDS coming in groups of three— first the TWO of SPADES, of DIAMONDS, and of CLUBS. Then the THREES, then the FOURS, then the FIVES, and then the SIXES.

The SOLDIER CARDS come next, in groups of twos— the SEVEN of CLUBS and DIAMONDS. Followed by the EIGHT of CLUBS and SPADES. Then the NINE of SPADES and CLUBS. Last, the TEN of SPADES and DIAMONDS

Now the ROYAL CARDS in groups of three— first the JACK, KING, and QUEEN of DIAMONDS, then SPADES, finally, CLUBS. The QUEENS no longer hold their Aces but rather scepters with their suit.

Last, the RED CHESS PIECES. Two BISHOPS. Two KNIGHTS, then the KING.

KING stops far SR. Turning back to witness the entrance of the RED QUEEN.

RED ROOKS: The Red Queen!

Then, in all her glory, the RED QUEEN enters. Like the WHITE QUEEN, she is dressed all in red, and resembles the chess piece for which she is named. Only the RED QUEEN holds the scepter for the Queen of Hearts. WHITE RABBIT follows just behind with four more RED PAWNS as GUARDS just behind.

RED QUEEN stops abruptly just before the CARDS on the floor. MUSIC halts.

RED QUEEN: Who is this?!

WHITE RABBIT: That is Alice, your majesty.

RED QUEEN: Not the girl! Who are these cards! Face down like that, I don't know if I'm looking at a five or a nine! Who are you?!

EIGHT: *(Popping head up)* We're no one, your majesty! *(Back down)*

TEN: *(Popping head up)* No one! *(Back down)*

SEVEN: We were just tending the roses, your majesty—

NINE: Not me— I was just walking by, and I tripped, yeah, that's it. I tripped.

RED QUEEN: My roses? *(Turning she sees the white roses. ANGRY!) My ROSES!*

I asked for Red Roses! Not only do you give me *WHITE* roses — but you attempt to deceive me with this *(she pinches a painted petal) RED PAINT?!*

EIGHT: *(Popping head up)* We're sorry, your majesty! *(Back down)*

TEN: *(Popping head up)* So Sorry! *(Back down)*

SEVEN: We were just trying to fix it, your majesty—

NINE: Not me— I was just walking by, and I tripped— I tripped!

RED QUEEN: OFF WITH THEIR HEADS! OFF WITH ALL THEIR HEADS!

ROSES and CARDS get up in a flurry— running away offstage. GUARDS calmly go after them. CARD QUEENS surround RED QUEEN trying to calm her and comfort her. WHITE RABBIT crosses to ALICE.

ALICE: Oh no! Poor things. It was just a mistake after all.
RED KING: *(Crossing to ALICE)* Oh don't worry, dear. I don't think she saw which cards they were. And she can't really afford to behead them all. As you can see, we're already a few cards short of a deck here.
ALICE: I did notice that. Why are there no Hearts?
WHITE RABBIT and RED KING shush her, checking to see if RED QUEEN heard. RED QUEEN doesn't notice.
WHITE RABBIT: There used to be all four suits of cards, Diamonds, Clubs, Spades, *and Hearts.*

During the following the RED QUEEN notices they're talking and slowly crosses to the conversation. ALICE, WHITE RABBIT, and RED KING don't notice until she is right next to them.

RED KING: But then one day, the Queen of Hearts said that *she* was the most beloved Queen—
WHITE RABBIT: Because *she* was the Queen of *Hearts.*
RED KING: Well, as you can imagine, the Red Queen did not like that one bit.

WHITE RABBIT: She had the whole suit wiped out, right down to the Ace.

ALICE: *(In a whisper)* She had them beheaded?!

RED KING: No one knows.

WHITE RABBIT: They were here one day, then gone the next.

RED KING: No more Queen of Hearts!

RED QUEEN: *(Standing right next to them, she announces loudly to all.)* I am the Queen of *all* hearts. *(To the trio)* Am I not?

RED KING: *(Nervous)* The Queen of my Heart, my love!

ALL: *(Variously)* Yes! Yes!...The Queen of ALL hearts!.... Yes!... Beloved Queen!

They continue to adore her until she stops them.

RED QUEEN: Alright, that's enough. It's time for croquet! *(All except ALICE, WHITE RABBIT and RED QUEEN exit to make preparations for croquet. After a beat.)* You know, Alice. It was very rude not to answer my invitation to croquet— why, you almost missed the game entirely.

ALICE: But I never got an invitation.

FROG FOOTMAN enters with the giant envelope, handing it to ALICE.

FROG FOOTMAN: An invitation from the Queen to play croquet.

ALICE: *(Turning to the QUEEN)* I accept?

RED QUEEN: That settles it! Let the game begin!

CARD QUEENS go to RED QUEEN and ALICE, bringing them pink flamingo croquet sticks, while the CHILDREN and SOLDIER CARDS assemble themselves into several arches. FROG FOOTMAN, the BIRDS, CHESHIRE CATS, KANGAROO, TWEEDLES, ROYAL CARDS, and other chess pieces including: WHITE QUEEN, WHITE KNIGHT, RED ROOKS, RED KNIGHTS, RED BISHOPS, and RED KING, come together to form a crowd, watching the game. CARD QUEENS join the other ROYAL CARDS in the crowd.

WHITE RABBIT: The Queen shall go first.

RED QUEEN takes a hedgehog ball from WHITE RABBIT, sets up her shot, pulls the flamingo back and—- suddenly, the CHEF bursts on stage, DSL.

CHEF: *(Shouting)* SOMEONE'S STOLE THE TARTS!

ALL Gasp and LIGHTS blackout for scene change.

Scene 6

LIGHTS come up on the Wonderland Courtroom. An eight foot tall podium made of cards acts as a judge's bench SR. Two benches on the tiered platform CS hold the jury: CHESHIRE CATS 1-9, TWEEDLE DEE, TWEEDLE DUM, and DODO.

Two more Benches hold the gallery of spectators SL, with the rest of the cast standing behind or on the thrusts. ALICE sits closest to the jury, and CHESHIRE CAT 1, with the WHITE RABBIT beside her. ALL are on stage, with the exception of MAD HATTER, MARCH HARE, DORMOUSE, CHEF, MOUSE and DINAH.

Two GUARDS stand on either side of the QUEEN of DIAMONDS and the JACK of DIAMONDS, DSR.

KANGAROO BARRISTER stands stage left of the podium.

ALICE: *(To RABBIT)* I've never been in a courtroom before. *(Pointing at the podium)* That must be where the judge will sit. *(Pointing at the platform)* Is that the jury there?
WHITE RABBIT: Yes, that is the jury. Twelve of Wonderland's finest citizens.
TWEEDLES wave excitedly.
ALICE: Yes… but wouldn't the cats count as one?
CHESHIRE CAT 1: *(To ALICE)* No. I told you. We live completely separate lives. We're nothing alike.

CHESHIRE CATS simultaneously lick the back of their paws, and stretch like the cats they are.

ALICE: Of course...how silly of me. *(After a beat)* Who will act as the Judge?

RED ROOK 1: All Rise!

ALL stand as RED QUEEN enters, instead of a scepter she now holds a large red gavel and wears a white judges wig under her red crown.

RED ROOK 2: The honorable and glorious Red Queen presiding!

RED QUEEN ascends her podium and sits. ALL sit.

RED ROOK 1: Court is now in session.

RED ROOK 2: Come forward and you shall be a bird.

ALICE: Oh no, not the Red Queen! The poor Jack of Diamonds is doomed. It's certain to be a death sentence!

RED QUEEN: Barrister, read the accusation!

KANGAROO BARRISTER: The Queen of Hearts, she made some tarts. All on a summer's day. The knave of Hearts, he stole the tarts, And took them quite away!

RED QUEEN: I've heard enough! Sentence him to death!

QUEEN of DIAMONDS: But I'm not even the Queen of Hearts! We're Diamonds!

RED QUEEN: Close enough!

QUEEN of DIAMONDS: My son didn't steal anything, your majesty! Please!

RED KING: *(From the Gallery)* Perhaps, my love, we should at least hear from the witnesses? For fun?

106

RED QUEEN: Oh, alright. Make your case, Kangaroo.

KANGAROO BARRISTER: I shall call my first witness: The Mad Hatter!

ALL gasp, except ALICE. MAD HATTER enters from SL with the MARCH HARE and the DORMOUSE just behind. MAD HATTER is visibly frightened. He holds a tea cup and scone, shaking the cup as he sips. The DORMOUSE leans on MARCH HARE, asleep on her feet.

MAD HATTER: I'm sorry your majesty, for bringing these into the court. You see, I hadn't finished my tea when I was called.

RED QUEEN: At this time of day? When did you start your tea?

MAD HATTER: *(looking back at Hare and Dormouse.)* March 14th?

MARCH HARE: 15th.

DORMOUSE: *(Awake)* 16th! *(Asleep.)*

KANGAROO: *(To jury)* Write that down.

Jury writes it down.

TWEEDLE DUM: *(To DEE)* How do you spell, "that?"

RED QUEEN: *(To HATTER)* Take off your hat!

MAD HATTER: I'm afraid, I can't.

RED QUEEN: Why not?!

MAD HATTER: It's not my hat.

RED QUEEN: Stolen?! Off with his head!

MAD HATTER: No, no— I'm a hatter. I *make* hats and sell them. So I don't actually own any hats of my own. This one's on sale. See? (*He pulls a large price tag out of the band, and tucks it back in again after a moment.*)

RED QUEEN: Overpriced, if you ask me.

KANGAROO: Where were you when the tarts were discovered missing, Mr. Hatter?

MAD HATTER: I, I, I—

RED QUEEN: Speak up now!

MAD HATTER: I, I, I—

RED QUEEN: Give your evidence, Hatter. And don't be nervous or I will have you executed on the spot!

MAD HATTER: I, I, I—

ALICE: Poor hatter!

RED QUEEN: Give your evidence or I will have you executed, nervous or not!

MAD HATTER: (*Shouts*) I was having tea!

ALL gasp!

MAD HATTER: I was having tea and then the March Hare said —

MARCH HARE: I did not!

MAD HATTER: You did!

MARCH HARE: I deny it!

RED QUEEN: He denies it!

KANGAROO: (*To Jury*) Write that down.

Jury writes it down.

MAD HATTER: Well, then...I suppose I was having tea. Although with tea time going on for such a long time, the bread was almost gone, the butter dish was nearly bare, and with the twinkling of the tea— I suppose that was where the trouble began—

RED QUEEN: The twinkling of the what?

MAD HATTER: It begins with the tea, your majesty.

RED QUEEN: Of course "twinkling" begins with a "T," what do you take me for?

QUEEN of CLUBS and SPADES stand up with the FOURs of CLUBS and SPADES hiding just behind them. FOURS stand facing the audience so their numbers can be seen.

QUEEN of CLUBS: Not the fours, your majesty!

QUEEN of SPADES: They're just children!

QUEEN of CLUBS: They didn't take anything!

RED QUEEN: Of course they didn't! Sit down, you flatheads! *(To HATTER)* If that is all you know, you may stand down, Hatter.

MAD HATTER: But your majesty, I can't get any lower. I'm already standing on the floor.

RED QUEEN: Then you may *sit* on the floor. Over there! *(She points to a spot DSL next to the gallery.)* And take these silly rodents with you!

MAD HATTER and MARCH HARE drag DORMOUSE to DSL and sit on the floor.

KANGAROO: My next witness is the Chef!

CHEF enters DSR.

KANGAROO: Chef, do you promise to tell the truth, the whole truth, and nothing but the truth, so help you cod?

CHEF: No.

KANGAROO: No?

CHEF: No.

KANGAROO: I'm done with this witness.

RED QUEEN: If there are no more witnesses, I will give the verdict.

KANGAROO: Just one more your highness, I call to the witness stand— Alice!

ALL gasp.

ALICE: *(Standing)* Me? *(She goes to the witness position right of the podium)* my name is Alice, and I promise to tell the truth. So help me cod.

RED QUEEN: And what do you know of the missing tarts?

ALICE: Nothing.

RED QUEEN: Nothing?

ALICE: Nothing whatsoever.

RED QUEEN: Nothing whatsoever?

KANGAROO: *(To Jury)* That's important. Write that down.

Jury writes it down.

ALICE: It doesn't matter, though. He clearly didn't steal the tarts.

KANGAROO: The rhyme states that the "knave," or Jack, stole the tarts. And we all know that Jacks are wild.

ALL murmur agreement.

110

ALICE: But don't you find it curious that he is the Jack of *Diamonds*, not Hearts? And we all know that the there is no Queen of Hearts, or knave, not since the Red Queen had them all wiped out. *(ALICE surprises herself, realizing what she said.)*

ALL gasp, then murmur to each other.

RED QUEEN: Silence! Rule Number 42 of the High Court of Wonderland: No witnesses under 3 inches tall! You are dismissed.

ALICE: That is a ridiculous rule! And this morning I was much more than three inches tall, more than three *feet* tall, for that matter.

RED QUEEN: Liar! Rule Number 43: No liars!

ALL murmur, starting to turn against ALICE.

MAD HATTER: She told me her name was "Very Sorry" not Alice.

ALICE: My name is Alice!

RED QUEEN: Impossible!

CHRYSANTHEMUM: She's a weed for sure!

PETAL: For sure!

ALICE: I'm not a weed— I'm Alice! And I'm not afraid of you!

RED QUEEN: Number 44: You're not allowed to be not afraid!

ALICE: But I'm not afraid!

RED QUEEN: That's it! CHANGE PLACES!

MAD HATTER, MARCH HARE, & DORMOUSE: CHANGE PLACES!

GUARDS switch the QUEEN of DIAMONDS and JACK with ALICE. Now, ALICE is accused and the QUEEN is the witness.

ALICE: What are the charges?!

RED QUEEN: Alice you are accused of being curious, impossible, and not afraid!

MOUSE runs in screaming with DINAH right behind. MOUSE hides in the crowd, while DINAH stops center stage, suddenly noticing where she is...

DINAH: Did I miss something?

RED QUEEN: Who are you?!

DINAH: I'm Dinah.

RED QUEEN: And do you know this *Alice*?

DINAH: Of course I do, I'm her cat.

KANGAROO: Your highness, I would like to call Dinah as my next witness.

ALICE: I really must object, your majesty! This Kangaroo court has gone too far! She is only a kitten! This is ridiculous!

KANGAROO: I object to her objection, your highness!

RED QUEEN: Yes, yes. Go ahead.

KANGAROO: *(To audience)* I may be a Kangaroo, but I always hold myself to the highest honors! Never ridiculousness! Yes! Above all, I hold myself with distinction and dignity! *(After a beat, KANGAROO comically hops across the stage, crossing in front of DINAH to DSR.)* Dinah, would you please take the witness stand?

DINAH goes to the witness position as QUEEN of DIAMONDS and JACK cross to the gallery.

KANGAROO: How long have you known the accused?

DINAH: The who?

RED QUEEN: Alice.

DINAH: Oh, Alice! I've known her my whole life.

KANGAROO: And would you call her *curious*?

DINAH: Oh yes, we have the greatest of adventures!

ALL murmur.

KANGAROO: Does she seem to do the *impossible* on these adventures?

DINAH: Oh yes! Just today she grew over a hundred feet tall, and made a river appear from nowhere!

ALL murmur louder.

KANGAROO: Last question Dinah, and this is very important, does Alice seem to you to be *not afraid*?

DINAH: *(Sincere)* Alice is the bravest girl I know.

Murmuring grows even louder.

TWEEDLE DEE: She's guilty for sure!

TWEEDLE DUM: Guilty!

RED QUEEN: Silence! *(Banging gavel)* Silence! *(ALL quiet.)* While this latest evidence is very damning— I think that we will drop the charges. After all, *(she laughs at ALICE)* she is *just* a girl.

ALL: *(Laughing, variously)* Just a girl… How silly!….She's nothing... She's just a girl!

ALICE angrily breaks away from the GUARDS pushing to center.

ALICE: So what if I'm just a girl. What are you— a flower, a mad hatter, a march hare? *(Turning to the QUEEN)* And you! You're nothing more than a chess piece. Just a bit of cold stone! *(ALL gasp)* I may be a girl now, but I will grow, I will learn, and I will love— what will you do but continue to play your game? Loving nothing more than *to win.*

ALL: *(Except RED QUEEN, variously)* She right...nothing more than a stone...just a chess piece!

RED QUEEN: You hold your tongue!
ALICE: I won't! *(Seeing a large butterfly overhead, she gets an idea)* You see, your majesty, if flowers can dance and sing, if playing cards can walk and talk—and if a caterpillar can shed her skin and become a butterfly— just what do you think a girl can do? *(After a beat)* Much more than a stone for sure.

ALL gasp!

WHITE QUEEN: Checkmate!
ALL: What?

During the following one of the GUARDS climbs up the back of the podium, steals the RED QUEEN's crown, and brings it down to ALICE. After that the chess pieces assemble next to ALICE bending down on one knee. Triumphant Music begins

114

to play for the cheers. MUSIC is cut abruptly when RED QUEEN shouts.

WHITE QUEEN: She's got you there, Red! Checkmate! And with a checkmate, that means Alice is now Queen! And according to Rule #65: A Queen is judged only by her character. And she's got that in spades! *(SPADES cheer! Crossing to stand next to ALICE.)* Three cheers for Queen Alice!

ALL: Hip-hip-hooray! Hip-hip-Hooray! Hip-hip-hooray!

RED QUEEN: *(Overlapping with the last Hooray, she's loud enough to outshout them all.)* HER?? *(After a beat)* Queen Alice?! What nonsense! What tripe! What—

TWEEDLE DUM: *(Standing up)* What's tripe, your majesty?

RED QUEEN: *(To TWEEDLE, then ALICE, then ALL)* Off with your head! Off with her head! Off with all your heads!

ALICE: That's enough of you, or I'll have you in a sack like the little chess piece you are! If I were my right size, you'd be boxed already!

RED QUEEN: *(With an evil smile)* But you aren't your right size, are you? Guards! Seize her!

RED CHESS PIECES— GUARDS and ROOKS stand up ready to grab her. ALICE slowly backs off toward SR. PIECES get closer and closer.

RED QUEEN: I may be a small chess piece, I may never grow up, but I have an army of pawns, and you do not!

CHESHIRE CAT 1: Perhaps you ought to do some of that growing now, Alice.

ALICE: What?

CHESHIRE CAT 1: The mushroom in your pocket! One side makes you larger! Remember!

PIECES chase ALICE off SR. Then we hear a slide whistle going up. PIECES come running back on, screaming. Then we see Alice's enormous shoe.

MOUSE: Run for your life! She's a giant!

RED QUEEN: Stand your ground pawns! Attack!

The following is absolute chaos: MUSIC blares. LIGHTS go wild, with colors and shapes. PIECES attack ALICE's shoe. As ALL characters run back and forth in a panic. CURTAIN closes as MUSIC and LIGHTS dim.

BEFORE the audience has a chance to clap, MUSIC stops, and LIGHTS come up on ALICE, asleep in her daisy field. She's kicking in her sleep, muttering about "flowers," "cats," "wonderland," and "cards." ADA enters.

ADA: Alice! Alice! Wake up, dear!

ALICE: *(Startling awake)* Twinkle, twinkle, little bat—

ADA: What was that?

ALICE: Nothing. *(After a beat)* Dinah! Where's Dinah?!

ADA: *(Holding out a stuffed cat, DINAH meows from offstage)* She's right here. You fell asleep during your lesson. I swear you could sleep anywhere. You're such a little dormouse.

116

ALICE: A dormouse? How silly, Ada. I've never heard of such a thing.

ADA: Come along, we're late.

ALICE: *(Standing up)* Late for what?

ADA: It's tea time, of course.

ALICE: Of course. *(She smiles.)* It's always tea time.

They exit together.

MUSIC.
THE END.

Made in the USA
Lexington, KY
13 July 2019